LEA♥E NOTHING UNSAID

A Step-by-Step Guide to Writing
WORDS THAT MATTER FOREVER

JODY NOLAND

LeaveNothingUnsaid.com

Dedication

In memory of the late Larry Elliott,
whose example inspired this dream.

With loving thanks to the many dear friends who have
prayed for me and encouraged me to fulfill this calling.

Soli Deo Gloria!

A Note from the Author

Bravo! Let me applaud you for taking a wonderful first step on behalf of the people you love.

There is no better time than right now to do this. As with many other vitally important tasks, it's easy to procrastinate about writing letters. Please, please don't let the busyness of daily life deter you.

The potential impact of a simple affirming letter is hard to measure. Yes, spoken words are important. But putting encouraging words into tangible form is a priceless gift.

My passion about the importance of these letters continues to grow as I hear story after story of their impact. I wish you could look into people's eyes, as I do, and see the tears of gratitude as they tell me about a letter they have received. Or see the longing for a letter that never came.

Why the watering can on the front cover? It's because I know that your words of affirmation, poured into the life of someone you love, can make a tremendous difference. Like water on a thirsty plant, your words can nurture life and growth in a loved one.

I recently heard the phrase "When you're inside the jar, you can't read the label." And that is so true! People often cannot see the positives about themselves that others can see.

My dream is a big one. Some might call it a "B.H.A.G." (Big, Hairy, Audacious Goal) I call it my God-sized prayer. I dream of cultivating a movement of people who are intentional about writing affirming letters to those they love. Words that matter forever.

Thanks for the privilege of helping you with this important task.

Table of Contents

· ·

The Inspiration

• •

The halls of Emory Hospital bustled with activity. As we wove our way through the maze, a sick feeling overcame me. "This must be a nightmare. How could this possibly be happening to Larry?"

Our friend had taken his family to Europe for a long awaited adventure. An amazing example of servant leadership, Larry had sold his successful insurance business several years before and had turned his life upside down to minister to hurting children. He and his wife Bev had gone from living a comfortable executive lifestyle to initially serving as house parents at a children's home in Alabama, and then helping to run a children's home near Atlanta. But this trip was for Larry's own family, and it was to be a special time with those dearest to him.

Now, at age 48, he faced surgery for a brain tumor. The flight to Italy had set off an excruciating headache. In Florence, a CAT scan revealed a brain tumor, and the family had immediately returned to Atlanta. The pilot even flew at a reduced altitude in an attempt to minimize the horrible pressure on Larry's brain. Surgery was scheduled for the next morning.

It wasn't hard to identify Larry's room. It was the one where people overflowed into the hallway because there was not adequate space for all the friends. As always, Larry was gracious and, not surprisingly, he was trying to comfort those who had come to comfort him. But there was also a great sense of urgency about him, as he asked Bev for pen and paper. I wondered what was so important that he needed to write.

Bev later told me what was so urgent. Larry wanted to write a letter of blessing for each of their three children – one in high school, one in college, and one already married – before he went into surgery the next morning, not knowing if he would survive. He did live for another 9 months after that surgery, and continued to be an amazing example of how to live **and** die with faith, integrity and courage.

Having their father's written words of affirmation has served as a tremendous source of encouragement and comfort to each of Larry's children as they have grown over the last 10 years. Here's what Larry's youngest daughter, Emily, has to say about the importance of that message from her dad:

"The note he wrote for me that night at the hospital is something I can go back to and remember not only how much he loved me, but also the short version of what he wanted me to know and become as I grew up and walked through life. Now, that note is a glimpse of the treasure of our relationship
for people in my life who never knew Daddy, like my husband Jake and our children."

In the same year that Larry died, two other friends in their 40s died suddenly. They had no warning. Both were pictures of health. Their deaths came as tremendous shocks. As I watched three grieving families, I thought about the comfort that Larry's written affirmations had provided to his family, and I thought about how much those other grieving families would loved to have had something similar. I especially hurt for the children, who knew unquestionably of their parent's love, but desperately missed the reassurance and security that their physical presence provided.

Like the comfort that a well-loved blanket provides to a child, words of affirmation seem to provide that to people of all ages. Over the last decade, I have felt an increasing desire to encourage everyone I know to "leave nothing unsaid." I cling to cards and notes I have from loved ones who have died, realizing those written words provide the most tangible reminder I have of that person's love for me and belief in me.

On September 11th and afterward, I wondered how many who had died had left any form of written blessing for their families and how much of a difference it would have made. I wonder the same thing when people die of cancer or heart attacks or car accidents ... have they left words of blessing and affirmation for their loved ones?

My dream is for every parent to prepare a letter of affirmation for each of their children and for other significant loved ones. In 2009 that desire became much more personal when my husband, Mike, was diagnosed with Stage 4 liver cancer. From the onset of the disease, I urged my husband to write letters to each of his children. Sadly, his illness was ferocious and he died three short months later, having never begun the letters. Shortly after my husband's death, one of my stepdaughters asked if her dad had written letters to the children … and it was heartbreaking to tell her "no."

What follows is my attempt to make this a simple process for you. The important thing is to **DO IT!** No one is going to grade you on your writing ability. What's important is to get your feelings in writing and to put them with your other important papers, i.e. your will. (And if you don't have one of those, you need to!)

Some have chosen to present their letters on birthdays or other special occasions. It's up to you! There are no "rules" other than that you need to get it done. If your children are still small, please still put something in writing. You can always re-write at a later point.

I realize that expressing these deep feelings does not come easily for some.
I commend you for doing this. You will never know the value to your loved ones.

Words of Wisdom

· ·

" How can you tell someone needs encouragement?
If he's breathing! "

> – Truett Cathy

" The bitterest tears shed over graves are for words left unsaid
and deeds left undone. "

> – Harriet Beecher Stowe

" Teach us to number our days aright, that we might gain a
heart of wisdom. "

> – Psalm 90:12

" The deepest human need is for appreciation. "

> – William James

" Only put off until tomorrow what you are willing to die having
left undone. "

> – Pablo Picasso

" A word aptly spoken is like apples of gold in settings of silver. "

> – Proverbs 25:11

4

Simple Guidelines

· ·

As you get started, here are some tips to follow:

- Express your heart.

- Be sincere and affirming.

- Don't use this as a platform to criticize, correct or apologize.

- Keep it simple.

- Finish. You can always revise it later.

- Be sure to sign the letter by hand. There's something about seeing a loved one's handwriting that opens a floodgate of emotions.

- Keep a copy with your will.

- There is no "right or wrong." The only "wrong" is not to do this ...now!

- Give without expectation of a response. Sometimes, words of encouragement need to marinate in a person's soul. You may never know the full impact. But you will always have the satisfaction of knowing you've left nothing important unsaid!

Appreciation vs. Affirmation

What's the difference between appreciation and affirmation?

> We appreciate what someone does
> **~We affirm who someone is**

> We appreciate someone's performance
> **~We affirm someone's character**

> We appreciate the outward things, i.e. appearance, success
> **~We affirm someone's intrinsic worth**

While both are important, appreciation is often about what the person does **for you**.

Affirmation is focused on **them**. When you affirm someone, you encourage his or her heart. You encourage the substance of a person … the things that do not vary with the rise and fall of the stock market or with the fickleness of public opinion, or the ravages of time.

Affirmation touches one's core.

Your List

● ●

Who are the significant people in your life that deserve a letter?

● Don't be overwhelmed by the number of letters you think you "should" write.

● Life milestones provide great opportunities to write letters.

● Milestones include: birthday, graduation, marriage, anniversary, birth of child, retirement, difficult season, move.

● Set a goal of writing one letter a month (Just think of the time you waste over the course of a month!). You can do this!

RECIPIENT	RELATIONSHIP	TARGET PRESENTATION DATE	MILESTONE

Focus on completion, not perfection!

LETTER OVERVIEW

• •

SECTION 1: Share Your Perspective
- What it has meant to you to be their parent (spouse, friend)
- Summarize your love and affection for them

SECTION 2: Affirm Their Uniqueness
- What is unique and wonderful about them?
- Character qualities, personality traits, temperament.
- God-given gifts and talents.
- What warms your heart about them?
- A special memory that highlights their uniqueness.
- Use a word picture to illustrate if possible!

SECTION 3: Share Your Hopes and Dreams
- Wishes and hopes you have for their life
- Encouragement for their spiritual journey
- Final words of wisdom ("Always remember this ...")

Most importantly...just do it!

Focus on completion, not perfection.

SECTION 1:

SHARE YOUR PERSPECTIVE

The purpose of this section is to provide a perspective about YOU. This is your opportunity to express what it has meant to you to be the person's parent (or child, spouse, friend, etc.); to put into words your love and affection. It can be short and sweet, but it's very important!

LEA♥E
NOTHING
UNSAID

SECTION 1:
SHARE YOUR PERSPECTIVE

• •

What has being this person's mother (father/spouse/friend/child) meant to you?

Examples:

- "One of my life's greatest blessings"
- "A daily delight"
- "A joy"
- "I feel like I won the prize when I got to be your mother"
- "Exceeded my greatest expectations"
- "I thank God daily for the gift of your life"
- "Because of you, my life is richer, fuller, sweeter, and more beautiful"

Now, in your words...

_____

_____

_____

_____

_____

_____

_____

_____

SECTION 1:
SHARE YOUR PERSPECTIVE
continued

• •

Summarize your love and affection.

Examples:
- "I love you with every fiber of my being."
- "No greater joy and fulfillment could God have blessed me with than you."
- "I never knew that I could love this deeply until I became your husband."
- "Being your mother has been one of the greatest delights of my life."
- "I'll love you forever."
- "I love you more than you could ever know."
- "I love you with no strings or conditions and I always will."
- "You are the light of my life."

Now, in your words...

_____

_____

_____

_____

_____

_____

_____

_____

_____

SECTION 2:

AFFIRM THEIR UNIQUENESS

This section is the heart of the letter! The purpose is to highlight what **you** see as the greatest attributes about the recipient, and why those qualities are so important. This is the essence of encouragement.

LEA♥E
NOTHING
UNSAID

SECTION 2:
AFFIRM THEIR UNIQUENESS

• •

WHAT SPECIAL QUALITIES DO YOU WANT TO AFFIRM?
Quickly circle all that apply. Then, review what you've circled
and select the 3 or 4 strongest attributes. Your next step will be to
describe the impact of those wonderful character qualities.

ACCEPTING	CONFIDENT	EXTROVERTED
ADAPTABLE	CONGENIAL	FAIR
ADVENTUROUS	CONSCIENTIOUS	FAITH-FILLED
ALERT	CONSIDERATE	FAITHFUL
ALTRUISTIC	CONSISTENT	FIRM
AMBITIOUS	CONTENT	FLEXIBLE
APPRECIATIVE	COOPERATIVE	FOCUSED
ARTICULATE	COORDINATED	FORGIVING
ARTISTIC	COURAGEOUS	FREE-SPIRIT
ASSERTIVE	CREATIVE	FRIEND
ATTENTIVE	CURIOUS	FRIENDLY
AVAILABLE	DECISIVE	FUN-LOVING
BENEVOLENT	DEPENDABLE	FUNNY
BOLD	DETERMINED	GENEROUS
BRAVE	DILIGENT	GENTLE
BRILLIANT	DIRECT	GIVING
BROTHERLY	DISCERNING	GOAL-ORIENTED
CALM	DISCIPLINED	GRACEFUL
CANDID	DISCRETE	GRACIOUS
CAREFREE	DISCRIMINATING	GRATEFUL
CARING	DRY WIT	HAPPY
CAPABLE	EASY-GOING	HARD-WORKING
CHARISMATIC	EFFERVESCENT	HELPFUL
CHARMING	EFFICIENT	HONEST
CHEERFUL	ELOQUENT	HONORABLE
CHRISTLIKE	ENCOURAGING	HOPEFUL
COMMITTED	ENERGETIC	HOSPITABLE
COMPASSIONATE	ENGAGING	HUMANE
COMPETENT	ENTHUSIASTIC	HUMBLE
COMPLEX	EQUITABLE	HUMOROUS

SECTION 2:
AFFIRM THEIR UNIQUENESS
continued

● ●

IDEALISTIC	PASSIONATE	SKILLED
IMAGINATIVE	PATIENT	SPIRITED
INCISIVE	PEACEFUL	SPONTANEOUS
INDEPENDENT	PEACEMAKER	STEWARD
INDUSTRIOUS	PERCEPTIVE	TALENTED
INNOVATIVE	PERSEVERANCE	TEACHABLE
INVOLVED	PERSISTENT	TENACIOUS
INTEGRITY	PERSUASIVE	TENDER-HEARTED
INTELLIGENT	PLAYFUL	THANKFUL
INDOMITABLE	POISED	THOROUGH
INITIATIVE	PRAGMATIC	THOUGHTFUL
INSIGHTFUL	PRAYERFUL	THRIFTY
JOYFUL	PRECISE	TIRELESS
JUST	PRINCIPLED	TOLERANT
KIND	PROMPT	TRANQUIL
KNOWLEDGEABLE	PRUDENT	TRANSPARENT
LEADER	REALISTIC	TRUSTING
LISTENER	REASONABLE	TRUSTWORTHY
LONG-SUFFERING	REFLECTIVE	TRUTHFUL
LOVING	RELIABLE	UNASSUMING
LOYAL	RESILIENT	UNDERSTANDING
MATURE	RESOURCEFUL	UNIQUE
MEEK	RESPECTFUL	UNUSUAL
MERCIFUL	RESPONSIBLE	VIRTUOUS
MODEST	RESPONSIVE	VISIONARY
MUSICAL	REVERENT	VIVACIOUS
NURTURING	SACRIFICIAL	VULNERABLE
OBEDIENT	SECURE	WELCOMING
OBJECTIVE	SELF-RELIANT	WILLING
OBSERVANT	SENSIBLE	WISE
OPTIMISTIC	SENSITIVE	WINSOME
ORDERLY	SERENE	WITTY
ORGANIZED	SERVING	WORSHIPFUL
ORIGINAL	SINCERE	

SECTION 2:
AFFIRM THEIR UNIQUENESS
continued

● ●

What were the traits that really jumped out at you? Pick the top three or four attributes, and write down why you think those qualities will serve him/her well in life, or how they have positively impacted you, your family, friends, or community.

Be sincere. Focus on what's unique and most special about your loved one.

Attribute: **Impact:**

_____   _____

_____

_____

_____   _____

_____

_____

_____   _____

_____

_____   _____

_____

SECTION 2:
AFFIRM THEIR UNIQUENESS
continued

• •

What warms your heart about this person?

_____

_____

_____

_____

_____

_____

_____

What especially happy memories do you have of him/her?

_____

_____

_____

_____

_____

_____

_____

SECTION 2:
AFFIRM THEIR UNIQUENESS
continued

• •

What unique gifts and talents do you see?

_____

_____

_____

_____

_____

_____

_____

_____

_____

_____

What makes him/her come alive? What is his/her passion?

_____

_____

_____

_____

_____

_____

_____

_____

_____

_____

SECTION 2:
AFFIRM THEIR UNIQUENESS
continued

• •

WORD PICTURES

Often, the most effective way to capture a person's uniqueness is through the use of a word picture. For some, images easily come to mind when they spend a little time focusing on a loved one's special qualities. For others, coming up with a word picture is extremely challenging.

To stimulate your creativity, here are a number of examples of word pictures:

"Being with you is like spending a day at the spa ... relaxing, refreshing ... I just don't want to leave!"

"You are like a summer garden bursting forth in fresh beautiful blooms every morning, every day."

"You are like a lighthouse. No matter how dark the night, I can always come to you for guidance and direction."

"You are like a fireworks display! Full of energy, full of color, full of beauty, full of excitement."

"You are like a stallion – strong, yet under God's control."

SECTION 2:
AFFIRM THEIR UNIQUENESS
continued

• •

WORD PICTURES *continued*

"You are like a bubbling mountain stream. You're fresh, full of life and enthusiasm."

"You are like a boulder – strong and unmovable. I can always depend on you."

"You are like a delightful golden retriever puppy. You're full of boundless energy, you're friendly and cute as can be, and you are so lovable! You never know a stranger, and everyone delights in your company."

"Watching you grow and develop has been like watching a beautiful butterfly. Each state of your growth and development has been wonderful and unique, and you have transformed into someone who is rare, special and beautiful."

"There are so many wonderful aspects of your character, that you remind me of a beautiful diamond with countless facets, all sparkling and reflecting light. Your good qualities are too numerous to count!"

SECTION 2:
AFFIRM THEIR UNIQUENESS
continued

• •

Stop and think about your loved one. Think about those unique character qualities that you identified. Now that you've read some examples of word pictures, does an image, a place, or something in nature pop into your head? If nothing comes to mind immediately, consider asking others who know the person well for ideas.

Ideas for Word Pictures:

_____

_____

_____

_____

_____

_____

_____

_____

_____

_____

_____

_____

_____

_____

SECTION 3:

SHARE YOUR HOPES & DREAMS

This section provides your opportunity to convey your "words of wisdom." If these were the last words you could say to the recipient, what would they be? What advice would you share? What things would you want them to always remember?

LEA♥E
NOTHING
UNSAID

SECTION 3:
SHARE YOUR HOPES & DREAMS

• •

What wisdom would you like to share? Are there some special
verses of Scripture you'd encourage him/her to
live by? (See pages 28–29 for examples)

Always remember this ...

_____

_____

_____

_____

_____

_____

What hopes and prayers do you have for his/her future?

_____

_____

_____

_____

_____

_____

SECTION 3:
SHARE YOUR HOPES & DREAMS
continued

• •

If you could give your child (spouse/friend) one or two pieces of practical advice, what would they be?

_____

_____

_____

_____

_____

_____

Is there a Scriptural blessing that you would like to use to close your letter? (See pages 30–31 for examples)

_____

_____

_____

_____

_____

_____

_____

THE FINISHED PRODUCT

. . . .

Now it's time to put the three sections together. You might want to hand write your letter or you might prefer to type it. That's really personal preference. But please be sure to sign it **by hand**. The sight of a loved one's handwriting, especially after they are gone, has a powerful impact.

You might choose to prepare this letter of love and affirmation and keep it with your important papers, such as your will. Perhaps you want your loved one to read this after your death.

My encouragement to you would be not to wait to share your heart. Your words of affirmation could make a tremendous difference **right now** in the life of your loved one, no matter what their age.

Several years ago, I wrote my dad a letter in honor of his 89th birthday. Fortunately, his mind was still keen. I was touched and humbled by how much he appreciated the letter. He told me what a treasure it was to him, and how he planned to reread the letter whenever he was having a bad day or felt discouraged. And I wondered ... why did I wait until he was 89 to tell him how much I cherished him? I'm so thankful that I had the opportunity to affirm my dad while he was still alive, and not just express my heart as a eulogy at his funeral several years later.

Just like you, I've had friends die unexpectedly from heart attacks, illnesses, car accidents and plane crashes. I've seen a loved one lose his earthly battle with cancer, having put off doing this until he

THE FINISHED PRODUCT
continued

• •

felt better, and that day never came. Only the Lord knows how many days each one of us will have on this earth. Please don't let the tyranny of the urgent keep you from completing something that will be a priceless treasure to someone you love.

"Teach us to realize the brevity of life, so that we may grow in wisdom." Psalm 90:12

• •

I would love to hear from you about how you have written and delivered your words of affirmation to those you love. Please email me: **jody@LeaveNothingUnsaid.com** with your comments and suggestions. Thank you for the privilege of helping you with this important task!

ATTACHMENTS

LEA♥E
NOTHING
UNSAID

WORDS OF AFFIRMATION FOR YOU

Many people have never received words of affirmation from their parents ... either verbally or in writing. And giving those words to those you love might seem especially difficult when you have never received them yourself.

However, each of us has received the ultimate Words of Affirmation – from our Heavenly Father, Almighty God. The Father's Love Letter© on the next page is a wonderful summary from God's love letter to us – The Bible.

I pray that these truths would penetrate to the depths of your heart.

AN INTIMATE MESSAGE FROM GOD TO YOU

• •

My Child,

You may not know me, but I know everything about you. Psalm 139:1 I know when you sit down and when you rise up. Psalm 139:2 I am familiar with all your ways. Psalm 139:3 Even the very hairs on your head are numbered. Matthew 10:29-31 For you were made in my image. Genesis 1:27 In me you live and move and have your being. Acts 17:28 For you are my offspring. Acts 17:28 I knew you even before you were conceived. Jeremiah 1:4-5 I chose you when I planned creation. Ephesians 1:11-12 You were not a mistake, for all your days are written in my book. Psalm 139:15-16 determined the exact time of your birth and where you would live. Acts 17:26 You are fearfully and wonderfully made. Psalm 139:14 I knit you together in your mother's womb. Psalm 139:13 And brought you forth on the day you were born. Psalm 71:6 I have been misrepresented by those who don't know me. John 8:41-44 I am not distant and angry, but am the complete expression of love. 1 John 4:16 And it is my desire to lavish my love on you. 1 John 3:1 Simply because you are my child and I am your Father. 1 John 3:1 I offer you more than your earthly father ever could. Matthew 7:11 For I am the perfect father. Matthew 5:48 Every good gift that you receive comes from my hand. James 1:17 For I am your provider and I meet all your needs. Matthew 6:31-33 My plan for your future has always been filled with hope. Jeremiah 29:11 Because I love you with an everlasting love. Jeremiah 31:3 My thoughts toward you are countless as the sand on the seashore. Psalms 139:17-18 And I rejoice over you with singing. Zephaniah 3:17 I will never stop doing good to you. Jeremiah 32:40 For you are my treasured possession. Exodus 19:5 I desire to establish you with all my heart and all my soul. Jeremiah 32:41 And I want to show you great and marvelous things. Jeremiah 33:3 If you seek me with all your heart, you will find me. Deuteronomy 4:29

AN INTIMATE MESSAGE FROM GOD TO YOU *continued*

• •

Delight in me and I will give you the desires of your heart. Psalm 37:4 For it is I who gave you those desires. Philippians 2:13 I am able to do more for you than you could possibly imagine. Ephesians 3:20 For I am your greatest encourager. 2 Thessalonians 2:16-17 I am also the Father who comforts you in all your troubles. 2 Corinthians 1:3-4 When you are brokenhearted, I am close to you. Psalm 34:18 As a shepherd carries a lamb, I have carried you close to my heart. Isaiah 40:11 One day I will wipe away every tear from your eyes. Revelation 21:3-4 And I'll take away all the pain you have suffered on this earth. Revelation 21:3-4 I am your Father, and I love you even as I love my son, Jesus. John 17:23 For in Jesus, my love for you is revealed. John 17:26 He is the exact representation of my being. Hebrews 1:3 He came to demonstrate that I am for you, not against you. Romans 8:31 And to tell you that I am not counting your sins. 2 Corinthians 5:18-19 Jesus died so that you and I could be reconciled. 2 Corinthians 5:18-19 His death was the ultimate expression of my love for you. 1 John 4:10 I gave up everything I loved that I might gain your love. Romans 8:31-32 If you receive the gift of my son Jesus, you receive me. 1 John 2:23 And nothing will ever separate you from my love again. Romans 8:38-39 Come home and I'll throw the biggest party heaven has ever seen. Luke 15:7 I have always been Father, and will always be Father. Ephesians 3:14-15 My question is… Will you be my child? John 1:12-1 I am waiting for you. Luke 15:11-32

Love, Your Dad

Almighty God

SCRIPTURAL ADVICE

· ·

"Trust in the Lord with all your heart and lean not on your own understanding; in all your ways acknowledge him, and he will make your paths straight." **Proverbs 3:5-6**

"Above all else, guard your heart, for it is the wellspring of life." **Proverbs 4:23**

"A generous man will prosper; he who refreshes others will himself be refreshed." **Proverbs 11:25**

"Commit to the Lord whatever you do, and your plans will succeed." **Proverbs 16:3**

"A good name is more desirable than great riches; to be esteemed is better than silver or gold." **Proverbs 22:1**

"Don't let anyone look down on you because you are young, but set an example for the believers in speech, in life, in love, in faith and in purity." **1 Timothy 4:12**

"Let your light shine before men, that they may see your good deeds and praise your Father in heaven." **Matthew 5:16**

"For nothing is impossible with God." **Luke 1:37**

"No eye has seen, no ear has heard, no mind has conceived what God has prepared for those who love him." **1 Corinthians 2:9**

"My grace is sufficient for you, for my power is made perfect in weakness." **2 Corinthians 12:9**

SCRIPTURAL ADVICE

• •

"For it is by grace you have been saved, through faith–and this not from yourselves, it is the gift of God–not by works, so that no one can boast. For we are God's workmanship, created in Christ Jesus to do good works, which God prepared in advance for us to do." Ephesians 2:8-10

"I urge you to live a life worthy of the calling you have received." Ephesians 4:1

"My God will meet all your needs according to his glorious riches in Christ Jesus." Philippians 4:19

"Whatever you do, work at it with all your heart, as working for the Lord, not for men, since you know that you will receive an inheritance from the Lord as a reward. It is the Lord Christ you are serving." Colossians 3:23-24

"Be joyful always, pray continually; give thanks in all circumstances, for this is God's will for you in Christ Jesus." 1 Thessalonians 5:16-18

"Humble yourselves, therefore, under God's mighty hand, that he may lift you up in due season. Cast all your anxiety on him because he cares for you." 1 Peter 5:6

BLESSINGS FROM SCRIPTURE

"May the Lord bless you and keep you. May the Lord make His face shine on you and be gracious unto you. May the Lord lift up His countenance upon you and give you peace." Numbers 6:24-26

"May He give you the desire of your heart and make all your plans succeed." Psalm 20:4

"May the grace of the Lord Jesus Christ, and the love of God, and the fellowship of the Holy Spirit be with you." 2 Corinthians 13:14

"And this is my prayer; that your love may abound more and more in knowledge and depth of insight, so that you may be able to discern what is best and may be pure and blameless until the day of Christ, filled with the fruit of righteousness that comes through Jesus Christ-to the glory and praise of God." Philippians 1:9-11

"Finally, whatever is true, whatever is noble, whatever is right, whatever is pure, whatever is lovely, whatever is admirable—if anything is excellent or praiseworthy—think about such things. Whatever you have learned or received or heard from me, or seen in me—put it into practice. And the God of peace will be with you." Philippians 4:8-9

BLESSINGS FROM SCRIPTURE

• •

"I have not stopped praying for you and asking God to fill you with the knowledge of his will through all spiritual wisdom and understanding. And I pray this in order that you may live a life worthy of the Lord and may please him in every way; bearing fruit in every good work, growing in the knowledge of God, being strengthened with all power according to his glorious might so that you may have great endurance and patience, and joyfully giving thanks to the Father, who has qualified you to share in the inheritance of the saints in the kingdom of light." **Colossians 1:9-12**

"May God himself, the God of peace, sanctify you through and through. May your whole spirit, soul and body be kept blameless at the coming of our Lord Jesus Christ. The one who calls you is faithful and he will do it." **1 Thessalonians 5:23-24**

"Now may the Lord of peace himself give you peace at all times and in every way." **2 Thessalonians 3:16**

More Ways to Encourage the Heart

· ·

Although using affirming words might seem awkward at first, it's a language we all can learn with some practice. Following are a variety of wonderful ideas for encouraging the people we love. Special thanks to those of you who have so generously shared your creative gifts.

Make a Word Cloud: When celebrating a special event such as a milestone birthday or a retirement, ask friends and family to provide one word to describe the person being honored. Those words can then be assembled into a Word Cloud (One word cloud application is www.wordle. net). It can be prepared as a poster in advance of the event (11 x 17 or even 8 x 10) or done "real time" and written with Sharpie by guests on a painted canvas.

A Mason Jar and Popsicle Sticks: For a special birthday, write an equivalent number of attributes you love about the person on popsicle sticks ("50 Things I love about you"). The sticks can be placed in the jar as though they were flowers. Tie a ribbon around the jar. You've created a wonderful gift with great meaning but low cost.

Christmas Eve Tradition: One couple shared a tradition they have been following throughout their many years of marriage. Each Christmas Eve, they go to separate parts of their home and write a letter to their spouse about the last year: the cherished memories, the things they love about their partner, and their hopes and prayers for the coming year. Then, they come back together and read the letters to each other. The letters are put in an envelope and placed with their Christmas decorations. At the beginning of the next Christmas season as the decorations are unpacked, the letters are reread. Then, they're saved with all of the previous year's letters. This couple has created a great memorial to their marriage and to God's faithfulness throughout the years.

Index Cards: Fancy isn't what matters. People want to know that their life has made a difference. When planning a special birthday party or anniversary event, ask guests to bring an index card with a sentence or two about what they really cherish about the individual in question. Some might want to share their sentiments at the party, while others might prefer to have their card included in a small album.

Photo Books or Scrapbooks: The content of a letter can be combined with photographs to make a wonderful gift! It's usually possible to find photographs that demonstrate the character qualities you've chosen to affirm.

Lunch Box Notes: For young children, enclosing an index card with a short note of encouragement in the lunch box can brighten every day. Use a fun sticker, a brightly colored card, and a short message like: "Of all the little girls in the world, I'm so glad that God let me be YOUR mom!"

Dry Erase Marker Note on the Bathroom Mirror: Start someone's day with an encouraging note and a smile. What better way to start the day than to be reminded that they are special and why? (Just make sure it's a dry erase marker!)

Family Vacations: Do you ever gather your extended family together for a week at the beach or the mountains? Make the week special by picking one or two people a day to be honored. Let that person choose the dinner menu and the activities for the day. Sitting around the dinner table, each family member can share one or two things that they really value about the person being honored. Even better…write them down on an index card so the person can look back over those encouraging words in the days to come.

Heart Happys: When celebrating a family member's birthday, have the rest of the family each express what makes their "heart happy" about the birthday honoree. Make it an annual tradition.

Windshield Notes: Looking for a creative way to love and affirm a teenage boy? Make a weekly habit of writing a note of encouragement and putting it under your child's windshield wiper every Friday morning. They might not say much about it…but it's a great way to tell a teenager that you believe in them.

Around the Table: Any time you gather a group of people around the dinner table, take the time to share something about each person that you especially love and value. It gives people a chance to get to know each other better and is a terrific way for people to feel cherished.

Writing a Card: Don't just rely on Hallmark to say it for you. Whenever you are writing a card, add a personal note. Tell the recipient at least one thing about them that makes them so special!

Something Girls Love: Here's a special gift idea for a college girl on a budget: make your friend a decorative jar that coordinates with her room. Put her name on the outside and then use pieces of patterned paper that coordinate with her room to write words of love and encouragement. You could also include special verses of Scripture. Curl the pieces of paper around a pencil and fill the jar with them.

Stocking Stuffer: Ever looking for something meaningful and creative to put in a special someone's Christmas stocking? Get a stack of cards and write down various things that you love about the person. Wrap the stack up and make it a stocking stuffer. You can count on the fact that those cards will be read and re-read throughout the year.

FORMS

SECTION 1:
SHARE YOUR PERSPECTIVE

• •

What has being this person's mother (father/spouse/ friend/child) meant to you?

Examples:
- "One of my life's greatest blessings"
- "A daily delight"
- "A joy"
- "I feel like I won the prize when I got to be your mother"
- "Exceeded my greatest expectations"
- "I thank God daily for the gift of your life"
- "Because of you, my life is richer, fuller, sweeter, and more beautiful"

Now, in your words...

_____

_____

_____

_____

_____

_____

_____

_____

SECTION 1:
SHARE YOUR PERSPECTIVE
continued

• •

Summarize your love and affection.

Examples:
- "I love you with every fiber of my being."
- "No greater joy and fulfillment could God have blessed me with than you."
- "I never knew that I could love this deeply until I became your husband."
- "Being your mother has been one of the greatest delights of my life."
- "I'll love you forever."
- "I love you more than you could ever know."
- "I love you with no strings or conditions and I always will."
- "You are the light of my life."

Now, in your words...

_____

_____

_____

_____

_____

_____

_____

SECTION 2:
AFFIRM THEIR UNIQUENESS

• •

WHAT SPECIAL QUALITIES DO YOU WANT TO AFFIRM?

Quickly circle all that apply. Then, review what you've circled and select the 3 or 4 strongest attributes. Your next step will be to describe the impact of those wonderful character qualities.

ACCEPTING	CONFIDENT	EXTROVERTED
ADAPTABLE	CONGENIAL	FAIR
ADVENTUROUS	CONSCIENTIOUS	FAITH-FILLED
ALERT	CONSIDERATE	FAITHFUL
ALTRUISTIC	CONSISTENT	FIRM
AMBITIOUS	CONTENT	FLEXIBLE
APPRECIATIVE	COOPERATIVE	FOCUSED
ARTICULATE	COORDINATED	FORGIVING
ARTISTIC	COURAGEOUS	FREE-SPIRIT
ASSERTIVE	CREATIVE	FRIEND
ATTENTIVE	CURIOUS	FRIENDLY
AVAILABLE	DECISIVE	FUN-LOVING
BENEVOLENT	DEPENDABLE	FUNNY
BOLD	DETERMINED	GENEROUS
BRAVE	DILIGENT	GENTLE
BRILLIANT	DIRECT	GIVING
BROTHERLY	DISCERNING	GOAL-ORIENTED
CALM	DISCIPLINED	GRACEFUL
CANDID	DISCRETE	GRACIOUS
CAREFREE	DISCRIMINATING	GRATEFUL
CARING	DRY WIT	HAPPY
CAPABLE	EASY-GOING	HARD-WORKING
CHARISMATIC	EFFERVESCENT	HELPFUL
CHARMING	EFFICIENT	HONEST
CHEERFUL	ELOQUENT	HONORABLE
CHRISTLIKE	ENCOURAGING	HOPEFUL
COMMITTED	ENERGETIC	HOSPITABLE
COMPASSIONATE	ENGAGING	HUMANE
COMPETENT	ENTHUSIASTIC	HUMBLE
COMPLEX	EQUITABLE	HUMOROUS

SECTION 2:
AFFIRM THEIR UNIQUENESS
continued

• •

IDEALISTIC

IMAGINATIVE

INCISIVE

INDEPENDENT

INDUSTRIOUS

INNOVATIVE

INVOLVED

INTEGRITY

INTELLIGENT

INDOMITABLE

INITIATIVE

INSIGHTFUL

JOYFUL

JUST

KIND

KNOWLEDGEABLE

LEADER

LISTENER

LONG-SUFFERING

LOVING

LOYAL

MATURE

MEEK

MERCIFUL

MODEST

MUSICAL

NURTURING

OBEDIENT

OBJECTIVE

OBSERVANT

OPTIMISTIC

ORDERLY

ORGANIZED

ORIGINAL

PASSIONATE

PATIENT

PEACEFUL

PEACEMAKER

PERCEPTIVE

PERSEVERANCE

PERSISTENT

PERSUASIVE

PLAYFUL

POISED

PRAGMATIC

PRAYERFUL

PRECISE

PRINCIPLED

PROMPT

PRUDENT

REALISTIC

REASONABLE

REFLECTIVE

RELIABLE

RESILIENT

RESOURCEFUL

RESPECTFUL

RESPONSIBLE

RESPONSIVE

REVERENT

SACRIFICIAL

SECURE

SELF-RELIANT

SENSIBLE

SENSITIVE

SERENE

SERVING

SINCERE

SKILLED

SPIRITED

SPONTANEOUS

STEWARD

TALENTED

TEACHABLE

TENACIOUS

TENDER-HEARTED

THANKFUL

THOROUGH

THOUGHTFUL

THRIFTY

TIRELESS

TOLERANT

TRANQUIL

TRANSPARENT

TRUSTING

TRUSTWORTHY

TRUTHFUL

UNASSUMING

UNDERSTANDING

UNIQUE

UNUSUAL

VIRTUOUS

VISIONARY

VIVACIOUS

VULNERABLE

WELCOMING

WILLING

WISE

WINSOME

WITTY

WORSHIPFUL

SECTION 2:
AFFIRM THEIR UNIQUENESS
continued

• •

What were the traits that really jumped out at you? Pick the top three or four attributes, and write down why you think those qualities will serve him/her well in life, or how they have positively impacted you, your family, friends, or community.

Be sincere. Focus on what's unique and most special about your loved one.

Attribute: **Impact:**

_____   _____

_____

_____   _____

_____

_____   _____

_____

_____   _____

_____

SECTION 2:
AFFIRM THEIR UNIQUENESS
continued

• •

What warms your heart about this person?

_____

_____

_____

_____

_____

_____

_____

What especially happy memories do you have of him/her?

_____

_____

_____

_____

_____

_____

_____

SECTION 2:
AFFIRM THEIR UNIQUENESS
continued

● ●

What unique gifts and talents do you see?

_____

_____

_____

_____

_____

_____

_____

What makes him/her come alive? What is his/her passion?

_____

_____

_____

_____

_____

_____

SECTION 2:
AFFIRM THEIR UNIQUENESS
continued

• •

Stop and think about your loved one. Think about those
unique character qualities that you identified. Now that
you've read some examples of word pictures, does an
image, a place, or something in nature pop into your
head? If nothing comes to mind immediately, consider
asking others who know the person well for ideas.

Ideas for Word Pictures:

_____

_____

_____

_____

_____

_____

_____

_____

_____

SECTION 3:
SHARE YOUR HOPES & DREAMS

· ·

What wisdom would you like to share? Are there some special verses of Scripture you'd encourage him/her to live by? (See pages 28–29 for examples)

Always remember this ...

_____

_____

_____

_____

_____

_____

_____

What hopes and prayers do you have for his/her future?

_____

_____

_____

_____

_____

_____

SECTION 3:
SHARE YOUR HOPES & DREAMS
continued

• •

If you could give your child (spouse/friend) one or two pieces of practical advice, what would they be?

_____

_____

_____

_____

_____

_____

_____

Is there a Scriptural blessing that you would like to use to close your letter? (See pages 30–31 for examples)

_____

_____

_____

_____

_____

_____

Rough Draft

· ·

**LEA♥E
NOTHING
UNSAID**

Rough Draft